41 All Natural Lung Cancer Meal Recipes:

Cancer-Fighting Foods That Will Help You Stimulate Your Immune System

By

Joe Correa CSN

COPYRIGHT

© 2016 Live Stronger Faster Inc.

All rights reserved

Reproduction or translation of any part of this work beyond that permitted by section 107 or 108 of the 1976 United States Copyright Act without the permission of the copyright owner is unlawful.

This publication is designed to provide accurate and authoritative information in regard to the subject matter covered. It is sold with the understanding that neither the author nor the publisher is engaged in rendering medical advice. If medical advice or assistance is needed, consult with a doctor. This book is considered a guide and should not be used in any way detrimental to your health. Consult with a physician before starting this nutritional plan to make sure it's right for you.

ACKNOWLEDGEMENTS

This book is dedicated to my friends and family that have had mild or serious illnesses so that you may find a solution and make the necessary changes in your life.

41 All Natural Lung Cancer Meal Recipes:

Cancer-Fighting Foods That Will Help You Stimulate Your Immune System

By

Joe Correa CSN

CONTENTS

Copyright

Acknowledgements

About The Author

Introduction

41 All Natural Lung Cancer Meal Recipes: Cancer-Fighting Foods That Will Help You Stimulate Your Immune System

Additional Titles from This Author

ABOUT THE AUTHOR

After years of Research, I honestly believe in the positive effects that proper nutrition can have over the body and mind. My knowledge and experience has helped me live healthier throughout the years and which I have shared with family and friends. The more you know about eating and drinking healthier, the sooner you will want to change your life and eating habits.

Nutrition is a key part in the process of being healthy and living longer so get started today. The first step is the most important and the most significant.

INTRODUCTION

41 All Natural Lung Cancer Meal Recipes: Cancer-Fighting Foods That Will Help You Stimulate Your Immune System

By Joe Correa CSN

To avoid lung cancer, good nutrition is a key factor and foods such as collard greens, broccoli, orange juice and seafood (especially cod) are the key ingredients. These foods in particular will help to give you the necessary nutrients and minerals that are helpful in preventing lung cancer.

Collard green leaves are full of sulfur containing compounds that support detoxification.

Broccoli. Broccoli is the only vegetable with a sizable amount of sulforaphane, a powerful compound that boosts the body's protective enzymes and flushes out cancer-causing chemicals.

Some researchers say oranges are a complete package of every natural anticancer inhibitor known up to now. Limonene in oranges can stimulate our antioxidant detoxification enzyme system, which helps to prevent and stop cancer.

While we often think of milk having vitamin D, we can also find high amounts in shrimp, salmon, and cod. Another good source are eggs.

Cod-liver oil is known to be rich in vitamin D which is a nutritional compound that is important when slowing down the growth of tumors and supporting the immune system. It is also rich in long-chain omega-3 fatty acids that are commonly found in oily fish. Omega-3 fats are healthy fats that also have protective properties against cancer.

41 ALL NATURAL LUNG CANCER MEAL RECIPES: CANCER-FIGHTING FOODS THAT WILL HELP YOU STIMULATE YOUR IMMUNE SYSTEM

1. **Collard Green Surprise**

Ingredients:

¼ cup extra virgin olive oil
1 16 oz. bag collard greens
2 cloves garlic
¼ teaspoon red pepper flakes
Pinch of salt

How to Prepare:

Boil collard greens in a pot of salted water for 5 minutes, then strain.
Heat olive oil and garlic in a sauté pan. When the garlic starts to cook add the collard greens, salt and pepper flakes. Sauté till well coated and the greens begin to fry in the oil. Serve warm or cold.

2. Super Green Eggs

Ingredients:

6 eggs
½ cup milk
¼ cup sour cream
¼ cup extra virgin olive oil
1 small onion
¼ cup cheese of choice
1 16 oz. bag collard greens
¼ teaspoons red pepper flakes
Pinch of salt

How to Prepare:

Beat the eggs, salt and pepper, milk and sour cream in a bow. Sauté thinly chopped onions in a skillet with one tablespoon of olive oil. Add the egg mixture and let cook slowly until the eggs are almost firm. Add the collard greens, cheese, and the pepper flakes. Fold the eggs over the collard greens and cook until the greens are soft and the eggs are firm.

3. Painted Beans and Greens

Ingredients:

1 can precooked pinto beans
1 16 oz. bag of collard greens
1 cup chicken stock
Pinch salt and pepper
1 tbsp. red pepper flakes
1 tbsp. olive oil
1 clove garlic
1 tsp. chili powder

How to Prepare:

Boil a pot of salted water and add the collard greens, boil till soft. Drain. In a skillet sauté garlic and oil. Add onions and cook until mixture is clear.
Add the chicken stock and add the pinto beans that have been rinsed and drained. Heat thoroughly and add the drained collard greens. Add the chili powder, salt pepper, and pepper flakes. Cook until the collards are soft.
This dish is also good served the next day after the flavors have blended.

4. Collard Green Salad

Ingredients:

1 16 oz. bag collard greens
1 bag mixed salad vegetables
1 tomato diced
1 red pepper diced
1 cucumber
1 red onion
3 tbsp. Herb flavored Olive oil (olive oil infused with rosemary and basil especially)
2 tbsp. Red Wine vinegar
Salt and Pepper to taste.

How to Prepare:

Combine all ingredients in a large bowl and mix.
Eat chilled.

5. Green Toast

Ingredients:

1 Loaf Italian Bread
1 tbsp. olive oil
1 clove garlic
1 tsp. parsley
1 tsp. basil
1 tsp. oregano
Pinch of salt and pepper
1 bag collard greens cooked and drained
1 lb. shredded mozzarella cheese

How to Prepare:

Slice Bread lengthwise. Using a pestle mash the spices and garlic with the olive oil until paste is formed. Spread the paste on the bread.
Strain the collard greens in your hands and dry with a towel. Remove as much moisture as possible. Layer the collard greens over the paste.
Add the mozzarella on top and broil until the chees melts. Eat warm

6. Green Pasta

Ingredients:

3 eggs
3 cups flour
1 cup water
1 tsp. salt
8 oz. collard greens cooked and drained.

How to Prepare:

Drain the collard greens after boiling until all the water is out of them.
In a mixer add eggs, water and salt. Slowly add the flour while mixing constantly on a low speed. When the dough comes together it is time to add the collard greens. Incorporate them thoroughly into the dough.
Let the dough sit for about 20 minutes covered with a damp cloth.
Using a pasta machine work the dough through the machine until the desired shape appears. Dry until ready to cook.

7. Green Pasta with Lemon Pepper Sauce

Ingredients:

Green Pasta
3 Lemons (One sliced into thin slices, two juiced)
1 tsp. black pepper
1 garlic glove
2 tsp. olive oil
¼ cup parmesan Cheese, Grated

How to Prepare:

Cook pasta in a large pot with salted water. Dry pasta should take about 6 minutes for an 'al dente' texture.

To prepare the sauce, sauté the garlic in the olive oil. Slowly add the juice of 2 lemons and the slices of one lemon. Add the salt and black pepper. Add 1 tablespoon of the grated cheese.

Add the al dente pasta to the skillet and add some the pasta water to combine as a sauce.

Add more parmesan cheese to your preference.

8. Green Soup

Ingredients:

1-quart chicken stock
1 16 oz. bag collard greens
1 cup cubed bread pieces
1 12 oz. bag of shredded carrots
1 small onion, minced
1 tbsp. minced garlic
1 tbsp. olive oil
¼ cup mushrooms, washed, sliced

How to Prepare:

Boil and drain collard green in a pan of salted water. Drain.

In a soup pan, add olive oil and sauté minced garlic, minced onion, and sliced mushrooms. Add the carrots and collard greens.

Add the stock to the pan and heat through. Add the cubed bread and serve.

9. Green Grilled Chicken Breast

Ingredients:

4 skinless chicken breasts
8 oz. collard greens boiled and drained
1 garlic clove, minced
1 tbsp. olive oil
2 slices mozzarella cheese
2 slices roasted red peppers
1 tsp. crushed red pepper flakes
Salt and paper to taste

How to Prepare:

Grill chicken breast until just about cooked. Remove from grill.
In a sauté pan add the minced garlic in the olive oil and add the drained collard greens. Add the pepper flakes. Remove from pan.
Transfer the chicken to the skillet and add the salt and pepper. Layer the collard greens, roasted red peppers and top with cheese. Cook until the cheese is melted and the wellness is to your liking.

10. Green Rice

Ingredients:

2 cups cooked wild rice
1 16 oz. bag of collard greens cooked and chopped
1-cup chicken stock
3 slices turkey bacon, chopped
1 can black beans, precooked
1 small onion chopped
1 glove garlic chopped
1 tbsp. olive oil
Salt and pepper to taste

How to Prepare:

Sauté turkey bacon, olive oil, garlic and onion. Add chicken stock. Season with salt and pepper and transfer to a large pan. To this large pan, add the precooked beans and cooked wild rice. Heat for 5 minutes, while stirring well. Add salt and pepper to taste, then serve.

11. Red and Green Salad

Ingredients:

1 bunch Broccoli stem cut off
1-cup cherry tomatoes
2 cups cooked tortellini
1 small can sliced back olives
1 small red onion
1 tbsp. olive oil
1 tsp. red wine vinegar
1 tsp. oregano
Pinch of salt and pepper

How to Prepare:

Blanch broccoli crowns, cut cherry tomatoes in half, drain olives, and chop the red onion.
Add the cooked tortellini and all ingredients in a large bowl. Toss with oil, vinegar and oregano. Add salt and pepper to taste. Chill before serving.

12. Broccoli Soup

Ingredients:

1 cup chicken stock
1 bunch broccoli stems removed
1 glove garlic, minced
1-cup heavy cream
½ cup cheddar cheese
1 small onion chopped
Pinch of salt and pepper

How to Prepare:

In a soup pan, sauté onion and garlic. Add the broccoli florets and continue to cook until the broccoli is soft. Add salt and pepper.

Add the chicken stock and boil at low heat. Add heavy cream and slowly warm the soup to high heat for 4 minutes. Add the cheddar cheese and slowly bring back to a low heat. Allow to cool, then serve at desired temperature.

13. Chicken, Rice and Broccoli

Ingredients:

2 cups cooked wild rice
2 chicken breast cubed
1 tbsp. Olive oil
1 Garlic clove, minced
1 broccoli crown
1 lemon, sliced
Pinch of salt and pepper

How to Prepare:

Clean broccoli crown and chop until the pieces are uniform. In a steamer add the broccoli and sliced lemon into the water. Steam for five minutes or until the desired level of softness of the broccoli.
Saute the olive oil with garlic in a pan and add the chicken cubes. Add the pinch of salt and pepper to taste. Cook for about 10 minutes until chicken shows no sign of pink and is completely white in the center of the cubes.
Add the broccoli crowns and toss with the chicken cubes.
In large bowl, pour over the wild rice, then serve.

14. Chicken and Broccoli

Ingredients:

4 chicken thighs
1 broccoli crown cut into florets
2 large russet potatoes, washed.
Salt and paper to taste
6 chipotle onions, minced
1 tsp. olive oil

How to Prepare:

Sauté the thighs to crisp the crust. Add to the baking pan with potatoes sliced into ¼ inch slices, and minced chipotle onions. Add salt and Pepper to taste. Add olive oil and the remaining oil from the sauté pan.
After 30 minutes in a 350 degree F oven, add the broccoli and toss to blend. Finish cooking until the chicken is cooked completely and the potatoes are soft, then serve.

15. Broccoli Cheese cakes

Ingredients:
1 crown of broccoli
½ cup grated Parmesan cheese
2 eggs
1 tsp. salt
1 cup flavored breadcrumbs
1 tbsp. olive oil

How to Prepare:

Steam broccoli florets in a water and lemon steamer. Allow to cool, then pulse in a mixer until the consistency of large breadcrumbs. Add eggs, cheese, salt and pulse again. When mixed add the breadcrumbs.
Heat the olive oil in a skillet. With an ice cream scooper, scoop out a portion of the broccoli/breadcrumb mix and flatten on the skillet. Fry until crispy on the one side and then flip. Fry on the other side until crispy. Serve with your favorite dipping sauce.

16. Broccoli Chicken Farfalle

Ingredients:
1 lb. farfalle pasta
1 broccoli floret
2 cups cooked chicken, squared
2 garlic cloves, crushed
2 tbsp. red pepper flakes
2 tbsp. olive oil
Salt and pepper to taste
Grated Cheese

How to Prepare:

While the salted pasta water is boiling, sauté the crushed garlic clove in olive oil in a frying pan. Add the broccoli floret and the squared, cooked chicken to the sauté and cook for 2 minutes, then set aside.

Cook the farfalle pasta until desired texture, then drain. Then combine the pasta, broccoli, and chicken together and mix. Top with the grated cheese and red pepper flakes, then serve.

17. Broccoli Muffins

Ingredients:

1 broccoli crown chopped fine
1 onion chopped fine
½ cup chopped carrots
6 eggs
½ cup cheddar cheese, shredded
2 cups flour
2 tsp. baking powder
1 tbsp. sugar
1 tsp. salt

How to Prepare:

In a large bowl beat the eggs. Add the vegetables and mix thoroughly. Add the shredded cheddar cheese, flour, baking powder, sugar and salt, and mix well.
Scoop into muffin cup baking tins.
Bake at 350 degrees F for 30 minutes.
Allow to cool and then serve.

18. Roasted Broccoli

Ingredients:

1 crown broccoli cut into florets
1 lemon, juiced
Pinch of salt and pepper
Pinch garlic powder
½ tsp. Chili powder
1-tbsp. olive oil

How to Prepare:

Preheat oven to 400 degrees. In a large bowl, toss broccoli florets with olive oil, garlic powder, salt, pepper and chili powder.

Place tossed broccoli florets on a baking pan and roast for 5 minutes. Then turn and finish roasting for another 3 minutes.

Remove from the oven, and allow to cool. Toss with the lemon juice, then serve.

19. Honey Orange Chicken

Ingredients:

2 chicken breast, cubed and dusted with flour
1 orange, juiced
1 tbsp. olive oil
½ cup honey
1 tbsp. sesame seeds
2 cups cooked rice of your choice
Pinch of salt and pepper

How to Prepare::

Sauté chicken cubes in olive oil to get a dark brown coating on the cubes. Transfer to a baking pan.
In a small bowl, mix the orange juice and honey. Add sesame seeds, then drizzle over chicken cubes.
Bake covered for 20 minutes at 350 degrees F or until the cubes are white and done in the center. Add salt and pepper to taste.
Serve over cooked rice of your choice.

20. Buffalo Style Cod Fish

Ingredients:

4 cod filets coated with cornmeal
¼ cup hot sauce
¼ cup warmed olive oil
Pinch of salt and pepper to taste

How to Prepare:

Warm the olive oil and hot sauce together in a saucepan. Dip the coated cod filets in the mixture and place on a baking sheet.
Brush remaining mixture to fully coat the filets.
Bake covered for 10 minutes at 350 degrees F. Serve with sides of choice, such as celery and carrot sticks with bleu cheese dressing.

21. Squash and Beet salad

Ingredients:

1-cup butternut squash roasted
1-cup beets roasted
1 green apple, chopped
½ cup pecans
2 cups arugula
1 cup orange sections
1 orange, juiced

How to Prepare:

Toss the arugula, green apple, squash, beets and pecans in a bowl. Add the orange sections. Dress with the orange juice. Chill to allow the flavors to infuse each other.

22. Orange Sections salad

Ingredients:
1 cup orange sections
1 sliced red onion
2 cups salad greens of choice
½ cup shredded carrots
1 cup sliced tomatoes
1 tbsp. olive oil
½ tbsp. balsamic vinegar
Salt and pepper to taste

How to Prepare:

In a large salad bowl, mix the salad greens, orange sections, onion slices, shredded carrots, and sliced tomatoes. Let them rest for a few minutes. In a small bowl, mix the olive oil and balsamic vinegar together, then toss over the salad, and serve cold preferably.

23. Orange Rice

Ingredients:

2 cups rice cooked of your choice
1 small onion chopped
1 small pepper chopped
1-cup broccoli in small pieces
½ cup shredded carrots
1 orange, juiced
½ tbsp. olive oil
Pinch of salt and pepper

How to Prepare:

Heat olive oil in a saucepan and add onions. Cook till onions are clear. Add broccoli, pepper, carrots and cook until tender. Add orange juice and heat for 1 minute. Add salt and pepper. Add rice to the saucepan and stir till well blended. Keep covered and cook on low heat for 5 minutes.
Serve warm. You may add a protein such as cooked chicken or cod, as your prefer.

24. Chicken al la orange

Ingredients:

1 roasting chicken with the inners removed and washed.
1 whole garlic glove
4 oranges, juiced
1 spring rosemary
3 basil leaves
1 tbsp. olive oil
Pinch of salt and pepper

How to Prepare:

In a crock-pot place half of the orange juice. Place the whole garlic glove, spring rosemary, and basil leaves in the cavity of the chicken. Place the chicken in the crock pot and add the salt and pepper. Pour the olive oil. Pinch small holes in the chicken and pour the other half of the orange juice over the top of the chicken. Let cook for six hours, then serve.

25. Citrus Lobster Salad

Ingredients:

1 cup of lobster meat. This can be frozen or removed from a fresh steamed lobster
1-cup orange slices
1 small red onion chopped
½ cup shredded carrots
1-cup arugula
2 tbsp. lemon juice
1 tsp. horseradish
2 tbsp. olive oil

How to Prepare:

In a large salad bowl, mix the arugula, orange slices, shredded carrots, and chopped onions. Add lobster meat on top of salad mixture.
Dress the salad lightly with olive oil, lemon juice and dot with horseradish, then serve.

26. Eggs and Avocado and Tuna

Ingredients:

3 hard-boiled eggs
1 avocado
Pinch of salt and pepper
1 can tuna in oil

How to Prepare:

Clean boiled eggs and chop. Clean out avocado and cut into bite size pieces. In a medium bowl, mix the chopped eggs with the avocado and add the tuna with the oil from the can. Mix lightly, adding the salt and pepper, then serve.

27. French Toast Bake

Ingredients:

8 eggs
½ cup milk
1 loaf of bread of your choice
1 tbsp. olive oil
½ cup maple syrup
1 tsp. vanilla extract

How to Prepare:

The night before soak the loaf of bread in milk and let it rest in the refrigerator overnight. When ready to prepare, place the soaked bread on a baking pan. In a medium bowl, beat the eggs with ½ cup of milk, add the vanilla extract and olive oil, and pour on top of loaf of bread to cover completely.

Bake at 350 degrees F for 10 minutes then remove from oven. Serve warm with maple syrup.

28. Egg Bake

Ingredients:

8 eggs
1-cup milk
1 pinch salt and pepper
1 package hash browns
1 package turkey sausage, precooked
1 small green pepper, chopped
½ cup cheddar cheese, shredded

How to Prepare:

In a baking pan, layer the sausage on the bottom, then layer the hash browns on top of the sausage.
In a medium bowl, beat the eggs, add milk, salt and pepper, peppers, and the shredded cheddar cheese. Pour onto the pan over the potatoes and allow seeping in between the potatoes. Bake for 10 minutes
This can be left overnight in the refrigerator and baked the next day or it can be baked at this point.

29. Italian Cod

Ingredients:
4 cod filets
2 boiled russet potatoes, peeled
1-cup green beans steamed
1 small red onion chopped
1 small red pepper chopped
1 clove garlic chopped
Pinch of salt and pepper
2 tbsp. olive oil
1 tbsp. red wine vinegar

How to Prepare:

Sauté the codfish in a frying pan with olive oil until it flakes apart. Slice the codfish filets into small flakes.
Dice the peeled, boiled potatoes into medium size cubes. Steam green beans to the crispness that you prefer, then allow to cool. In a large bowl, mix the green beans, potato cubes, onions, chopped peppers and chopped garlic.
Add the cod filets flakes and toss with olive oil and vinegar. Serve warm or cold.

30. Egg Soup

Ingredients:

2 cups chicken stock
2 eggs
½ cup Parmesan cheese
½ cup shredded carrots
¼ tsp. garlic powder
¼ tsp. salt and pepper

How to Prepare:

Heat chicken stock with shredded carrots until it boils. Add salt and pepper.
In a small bowl, beat the eggs and add to the boiling chicken stock while stirring. Boil for 2 minutes, then add Parmesan cheese. Remove from heat and serve at desired temperature.

31. Egg Salad Stuffed Tomatoes

Ingredients:

6 hard-boiled eggs, chopped
1 avocado chopped in small pieces
½ cup sour cream
1 chopped onion
½ cup chopped celery
½ cup chopped carrots
1 lime, juiced
4 medium size tomatoes cored

How to Prepare:

In a medium bowl mix the chopped eggs with the chopped onion, carrots and celery. Then add the avocado pieces and pour the lime juice into the bowl. Dress with sour cream, then stuff each of the tomatoes with the filling and enjoy. May add salt and pepper to your taste.

32. Frittatas

Ingredients:

8 eggs
½ cup milk
1 small onion chopped
1-cup mozzarella cheese, grated
½ cup mushrooms sliced
½ cup red pepper strips
1 baked potato
2 tbsp. olive oil
¼ cup parmesan cheese

How to Prepare:

In a large mixing bowl whisk the eggs, add a dash of salt and pepper and Parmesan cheese.
In a large saucepan with olive oil, add the onions and sauté. Add the mushrooms, red pepper strips and sauté till slightly tender. Add a pinch of salt and pepper to your taste. Pour the egg mixture to the saucepan and gently stir. Top with grated mozzarella cheese. Bake at 350 degrees F for 5 minutes then serve and enjoy.

33. The Best French toast

Ingredients:

1 loaf of bread
4 eggs
½ cup milk
Dash of salt and pepper
½ tsp. vanilla extract
2 tbsp. olive oil
½ tsp. cinnamon
¼ cup maple syrup

How to Prepare:

Pour the olive oil on a large frying pan and place on medium heat. Whisk the eggs, milk, salt and vanilla together in a medium bowl with a flat bottom. Slice the loaf of bread into ½ inch thick slices. Dip each slice into the egg mixture on the flat bottom allowing it to rest in the mixture on both sides for 2 seconds. Then place each dipped bread slice on the large frying pan and cook until they are light brown on both sides and set aside. Serve with maple syrup or cinnamon and enjoy.

34. Cod Fish Special

Ingredients:

1 lb. of codfish filets
1 tbsp. olive oil
1 lemon, sliced
½ cup of capers
1 sliced onion
1 small can of black olives sliced
1 small tomato sliced
Flour to coat the filets

How to Prepare:

Line a large baking dish with the cod filets that have been coated with flour. Place the sliced onion, black olives, tomato slices, capers on top and around the cod filets and then drizzle everything with the olive oil.
Cover with aluminum foil and bake for 10 minutes at 350 degrees F. Remove foil and bake for another 2 minutes. Serve warm with lemon on the side.

35. Stuffed Cod

Ingredients:

6 cod filets
1 cup cooked spinach
1 cup bread crumbs seasoned
½ cup Parmesan cheese
1 egg
1 lemon, sliced
1 tbsp. olive oil

How to Prepare:

In a medium bowl, mix the cooked spinach with the seasoned bread cubes, egg, and parmesan cheese until uniform and firm texture is reached. Spoon out a tablespoon of the spinach mixture and place on the center of each fillet. Carefully wrap the filet around the mixture. Place in a large oven pan and drizzle with olive oil and hint of salt and pepper. Bake for 15 minutes at 350 degrees F. Cod should flake when touched with a fork. Serve with lemon on the side and enjoy.

36. Orange Cod

Ingredients:

4 cod filets
1 sliced blood orange
½ tsp. garlic powder
1 tbsp. olive oil
Hint of salt and pepper
1 lemon, sliced

How to Prepare:

Arrange the cod filets on an 8 x 12 baking dish. Add a hint of salt and pepper and garlic powder. Sprinkle with olive oil and bake for 8 minutes at 350 degrees F. Remove from oven and top with the slices of blood orange. Complete cooking for 2 additional minutes until cod flakes when touched with a fork. Serve with lemon on the side and enjoy.

37. Baked Cod Fish

Ingredients:

4 cod filets
1 tbsp. olive oil
1 small tomato, sliced
1 small lemon, sliced
1 tsp. chili powder
Hint of salt and Pepper

How to Prepare:

Layer filets in a baking dish and cover with slices of tomatoes, onion, and lemon.
Drizzle with olive oil and salt, pepper and chili powder. Bake uncovered for 10 minutes at 350 degrees F.

38. Tuna Melt

Ingredients

1 can of tuna, in oil
4 slices mozzarella cheese
1 sliced tomato
4 Croissants
1 tsp. olive oil

How to Prepare:

Heat the olive oil on a skillet on low heat. Slice the croissants and place the bottom slice on the pan with the tender area facing up. Spread each of the 4 croissant bottom slices on the tender side with a slice of mozzarella cheese, a slice of tomato, and tuna. Then drizzle some olive oil on top. Cover each bottom slice with the top slice of the croissant and flip holding both side of the sandwich. Cook until the cheese melts and enjoy.

39. Turkey pepperoni Egg Scramble

Ingredients:

4 eggs slightly beaten
¼ cup milk
6 slices turkey pepperoni, precooked
1 small pepper diced
1 small onion chopped into small pieces
1 tbsp. olive oil
Salt and pepper

How to Prepare:

In a small bowl, beat the eggs. Then heat the olive oil on a medium-sized frying pan at low heat. Sauté the onions, peppers, and turkey pepperoni slices until tender. Add the eggs and the milk, and mix in the pan until uniform. Cook until egg scramble is tender to your taste.

40. Cod Potato Salad

Ingredients:

4 cod filets cubed
2 baked potatoes, cubed
1 small onion sliced
1 cup mixed sweet peppers sliced
1 tbsp. olive oil
1 cup celery, washed and chopped
Pinch of salt and pepper

How to Prepare:

Sauté onion and peppers in olive oil until the onions are clear. Add salt and pepper. Mix well. Add cod cubes and cook until the cod flakes at the touch of a fork.

In a large salad bowl, combine the baked potato cubes, chopped celery with the cooked cod cubes, and serve hot or cold as per your preference.

41. Egg Battered Cod

Ingredients:

2 eggs
¼ cup cornmeal
1 tsp. Italian Seasoning
4 cod filets
1 tbsp. olive oil
1 lemon, wedges

How to Prepare:

In a medium bowl, beat the eggs and add cornmeal and Italian seasonings. Mix well. Mixture will be thick but liquid.
Coat the cod filets with the egg mixture.
Heat the olive oil in a large frying pan and add the coated cod filets. Cook on medium heat until the egg mixture on the cod filets turns a light brown. Serve with lemon wedges and enjoy

ADDITIONAL TITLES FROM THIS AUTHOR

70 Effective Meal Recipes to Prevent and Solve Being Overweight: Burn Fat Fast by Using Proper Dieting and Smart Nutrition
By
Joe Correa CSN

48 Acne Solving Meal Recipes: The Fast and Natural Path to Fixing Your Acne Problems in Less Than 10 Days!
By
Joe Correa CSN

41 Alzheimer's Preventing Meal Recipes: Reduce or Eliminate Your Alzheimer's Condition in 30 Days or Less!
By
Joe Correa CSN

70 Effective Breast Cancer Meal Recipes: Prevent and Fight Breast Cancer with Smart Nutrition and Powerful Foods
By
Joe Correa CSN

www.ingramcontent.com/pod-product-compliance
Lightning Source LLC
Chambersburg PA
CBHW052127070526
44586CB00016B/2111